Prophetic
Wake Up It's Time To Cultivate

SpitVerb Entertainment LLC

J.L.Davenport

Copyright © 2008, 2013 by Jamelle Davenport
All rights reserved. This book, or parts thereof,
May not be reproduced in any form whatsoever
unless permission is received from author and/or
representative.
ISBN: 978-0-6151-7324-5

J.L.Davenport

Contents

Wake Up It's time To Cultivate

Note from Author

    I. Oppression

1. Eden
2. I is you
3. One amongst Many
4. Superiority
5. Oppressor
6. Egregious
7. False Offering
8. Hell, Take back your Devils

    II. Recognition

9. Why Do You Love Me So?
10. Rollercoaster
11. Howls of Pain
12. Mother Nature
13. Quiet Lonesome
14. Faces on the Wall
15. Deal with the Devil
16. We Are Sleeping
17. Beautiful One
18. Grab Hold of Today
19. Recreational

20. Emasculate

21. No One Helped

22. Nigga

23. BLACK

24. Celebrity

25. Recreate This Image

26. Drunk

27. Mask of Beauty

28. Give up Self

29. Suffer Blessed One

30. Reflection

31. Unique

32. Happiness Won't Come To You

33. He Made Me Feel

34. Kids Sing

35. Last Cry

    III. Sight Sound and Movement

36. True Art

37. Music

38. Good Morning

39. Thunderous Music

40. Dance

41. Feel the Pain, a compilation of Prison Song and Emasculate (Poems in Fanatical Kink Spoken)

About Author

It's Time To Cultivate

Note from Author

We all have to live together we have been learning for a long time; life is all about learning. We are all different that is why the world is so beautiful and so sad. We give birth we bleed we all feel pain we all love sometimes we hate we all want to be happy sometimes we are sad we all live and we will all die.

This work of expression is all about the observations of what I have witnessed in the modern world; the modern human. This expression is what I want to share with you.

J.L.Davenport

CHAPTER 1
Oppression

Eden

Once the world was dark

Then came light to diminish the night

In that light came forth the colors of the world

Wondrous colors

Peaceful and rich

Of nature, beast, woman and man

For the plan was a portrait to an eye

Mesmerized by thought and artistry

I is you

I is you

You is me

We together are creation

Creation gathered in form

The creators' breath is molding

How colorful

How beautiful

Wild, intricate and defined

What do you see?

No paintbrush begat the beauty

No, pencil and no pen

No camera to lock it in

No thought could master

J.L.Davenport

We are the image of the creator
Why do we look for the first race when there is none we created this complication
There are only nations and different tongue a lesson we shall suffer because...
They built a building to reach the heavens when they were close the creator brought it down
With the falling, confusion found its home; it says so in the bible where it is shown
What difference is there but none we are one The Creator made the materialization we in return destruct the manifestation
The thought was beautiful; to bring it life was awesome to maintain is heartache
Beauty can never stay

One amongst Many

The knowledge is too great for one to comprehend
The negative philosophy that has become a physical, political demon
Amongst those of us, who would and will try to lessen the impurities of this government
That is our barrier to sanity
One cannot contain the manifest of wrong that comes with the territory of being amongst... of having to identify with these cold hearted, unpredictable and by societies standard, evil
One can sew stars on a sheet, boredom is sometimes a blessing and yes, it is a work of art
Although the ideology of it all is teach, tell and be told that is how it goes
Deny, deal or die, when not yet civilized
Which means lose your culture, lose your pride, and throw away your religion
Unless it is abundant with wealth and looks good on TV
Run from old practices and hide under new ones, new ways, and new people
New people from different continents who will demand this adaptation
And get it

J.L.Davenport

Then snicker difference into your face
The knowledge is too great for one to comprehend
and in many ways; you are always one amongst many

Superiority

You take a man and tear him down
You tear him down until it becomes a norm
This becomes normality
Normality he passes to his seed
And
That seed passes to his seed
And
Each seed is ignorant because of the first error
Each is torn down, worn, scorned, and less than an animal
Ignorance, fear, isolation, and torture…
These all in combination brought upon the revelation…
The superiority of the other man

Oppressor

There is one oppressor, although it comes in a multitude of forms
Forms being a mold of shapes and sizes
Conditions and habits
Acceptance because of the past performance
It is of one color, one mind, and one act
It is a magnitude of hate
That has now become too great, too great because it is continually revised and reused to oppress
Oppress being to keep down unjustly... not allowed to touch the pedestal... limiting
It is a secret, but not very secret
Great minds can see truth within the hints and flaws overtime
One oppressor would show hate without guilt, without shame
One oppressor to diminish the numbers in a race
With the propaganda of fear and inferiority
The shadow; Christianity
The lie; Godly

J.L.Davenport

Egregious

Always there is one will not hide their hate, pain or glory
That one, will show it for the entire world to see
That one, will triumph to the top
Like a god and triumph even when falling
That one, the world will adore
That one, the world will follow
That one, the world will kill for
That one, the world will despise…someday
The world will try to analyze and depict…that one
However, that one will shine always one of fame
Egregious

False Offering

Through the many blessings, there is always a false offering
An offering only a mother could love
No one will notice him and he does not show himself
He grows with pain and no real glory
Eventually hate is his friend
Wicked coward to be a leader, a teacher
Statistician trickery to account for his trophies

His name will know the top for hundreds of years; his seed will glory in riches

We know him today

We fear his seed

We strive to overcome, to rise, to sit beside them as equal

We allow him immortality... and he said he would have it

Hell, Take Back Your Devils

There are devils all around, too many damn devils

Pale, deceitful, drunken, perverted, murderous, sneaky devils

On the right

On the left

In front

In back

In dreams

In the blood

Devils treading across, around and into the well-beings of good

With their pale mischievous ways

Hell, take back your devils, there is plenty room

CHAPTER 2
Recognition

Why Do You Love Me So?

Pain engulfing my soul I question
Why do you love me so?
He says, one-time visitor converted into a long-time customer
Come to church to receive your blessing or call my name and I will answer just the same
We can talk it out or we can shout
We can cry or we can sing
We can laugh and then we will dance
I am truly all you need.

I visit for answers
You tell me what I know
The answer is what I need

He says, I love you so because you have many questions and all the answers
Are you ready for a blessing?

Thank you Lord, I feel the blessing
I know you love me so, more than I will ever know
Thank you

J.L. Davenport

Rollercoaster

Rollercoaster's were always my favorite ride

I would sit in the back and be ready to fly

I could always see ahead of me

Everyone's faces changing expressions

When the ride would end

All the chaotic commotion

The silly behavior

Laughing, crying, being sick

I could see it all before exiting my seat

Then I would run and get in line for another chance to ride

But

This ride would take me on a journey

The journey to the front seat

The front seat

The front seat where nothing is in front of me but sky

I cannot see behind me

I cannot hear anything but screams

Screams

Screams of emotional breakdown

The wind is slapping me

I cannot breath

I've smoked too much of something tonight

I've drank too much of something tonight

I was having fun until I took flight

Laughing, then crying, then sick....Am I dying?

The silly behavior

Quiet

I feel like I am alone on this rollercoaster

Flying, everything flying

The wind is beneath my skin contorting it, changing it

The wind is in my hair...on this rollercoaster my life is continuously being shown

But

I cannot see behind me

I cannot hear anything but screams

J.L.Davenport

Howls of Pain

Distant howls of pain, lifted by gravity
Have traveled far to greet me
To share a story unbelievable
Inexcusable
However, at this moment I am all ears
For I am reassured to have something near to me who is also suffering
Selfish, maybe
Though human
Distant howls of pain tell to me your story; I will listen but may not hear
I will not care I am just happy you are here, miserable as you are
By far, you are the new best friend I have
Distant howls of pain do not cry
Though it may make you empty your pain, it only makes me swallow my shame
You are weak!
How sad is the yearning of your soul, I would love to comfort you, but it is pleasurable to see you suffer
I have no pity for you... I pity myself
You are making me strong; you are an excuse for my hardening heart.

If you are like me and I like you, then I have been reality and not undue

Although my heart is not cruel

Maybe it is the stresses in the day

Maybe it is the pollution or the way the earth turns

That has caused my inhumane hindrance

Excuses, excuses

Most times my thoughts are callous

Although the turmoil produced in my brain has yet to cause another physical pain

Maybe emotional drain or mental strain but never physical, never that

Distant howls of pain. Distant howls of pain.

You are too close, very close, like in me

The memories you bring with you are austere

Like a copy to my shadow

You have not traveled far after all

You have been with me from the beginning

J.L.Davenport

Mother Nature

The moon in the sky seems distant
So distant that it illuminates its glowing, hazy view
even in you
From whole to half
In your river its reflection shines
Cast off the flowing waters where it is renewed
Complete again
It is more beautiful

Quiet Lonesome

We find serenity amidst a quiet lonesome
Solace in our imagination
Faith in our visions
An absolute down drift of tensions that are easy to mention, seeming the tensions were building, and building on suspensions in time
Blinding us into a cloudy space
Although this cloudy space is easily erased
Into a laced place covered in images and memories
It is that quiet, haze where one single blink can remove the grace of this seldom-ventured place
Where the value of being alone will lose its

greatness and the complications of the present will creep upon thou swollen with a lonely grief

Faces on the Wall

I see you

Faces on the wall

Invisible to others but I see them all

I see them

I look away and look back and I see them

Can't get them out of my head

One end of my mind to the other

A man

A woman

Someone grinning

One so beautiful

I get my pencil and begin to sketch

I am lost within myself

Find myself I must

Get away from the wall

Too many faces

Run...no

Hide...no

Staring at those faces on the wall

Invisible to others but I see them all

They see me

J.L.Davenport

Deal With the Devil

Have you seen my skin?

My glistening black skin

My earthly brown

My moon stained yellow skin

My skin as tinted as nature

Camouflaged

I can adapt to any environment

God blessed me with this ability

Multiple colors for a multitude of people

But,

You devil are like opal

Your paleness is like scars across my heart

Your sight is like acid in my eyes

The thought of you devil, reeks at my soul

Torture does not allow my spirit peace

You must change everything, sunburned sour fruit

You are diseased mentally but somehow you succeed

Let me dislike you infinite

We Are Sleeping

The world created beautiful through us, in us and around us. Yesterday was yesterday. Black man stood strong, black man stood together, black man we shall overcome said Martin, and so shall we prosper. Today is today. Black man stand strong when trouble is near, black man stand together when profit comes in return, black man we shall overcome, we already did and prosper we do but at what cost? Today as black alone we are our own demise and today are fewer tears than yesterday.

J.L.Davenport

Beautiful One

The sun's colors reflecting off the big white clouds
In that, those clouds become beautiful and noticeable
If for one moment it should rain
The beauty of the sun cannot sustain
Big white clouds get cloudy and gray
Disturbing the balance of the beautiful one
Beautiful one let your colors shine brighter
However, the sun, feeling dirty will shy away and let the moon end the day
Tomorrow will be brighter as the sun awakens and those big white depressing clouds will disperse
Sun and sky
Blue and wide
Show beautiful colors

Recreational

The crickets are communicating

No matter

She is alone lost in chains

The chemistry of the drink; through her body it is expressing

All the impish thoughts reflective in her movements

Smoke in the bottle still and gray the ashtrays are empty

The room vibrating with music and loins are ready to participate

The crickets are communicating

No matter

She cannot hear them anyway

Her body is hot, her skin is radiant, and her hair is wild

Lips puckered and wet; she is singing

Then she is moaning no position is suitable for her mood

She is feeling hazy the drink is slipping through her fingers

Her grip is weak as her vigor is unbecoming

Just as the wild would appreciate, she is now ready to play

J.L.Davenport

The night will be long as steadily growing bamboo
The crickets are communicating
No matter
She is alone lost in chains
Sullied
Her voice will fade in the midst of pandemonium
Against one limb to the other
Where once was a drink; there will be another
In the pulling of her hair, if she was not limber
then she will be
Until the night is over
In the calm of a trashy room and floating aromas
Booze, smoke, and arse
A recreational concoction

It's Time To Cultivate

Grab Hold of Today

Stretch out your hands and grab hold of today

Tomorrow is not reachable

The future can be dreamed

Shot in the head

Now she is dead

A mother of five is not alive

Does your erection feel bigger?

So easy to pull the trigger

Deep does the knife penetrate; five times, it draws

its lines across warm flesh

Breathe deep the fluids of your lover as she withers

Does your erection feel harder?

Male fungus

Beat that bitch like a man

Hunt her down as if she is game

Fuck her and then choke her, let her bulging eyes

have the last breath

Did you have release?

Women outnumber and every day we increase

Because you devour your population like animals

now you come after us

First disease

Now guns and knives

I do not really exist

J.L. Davenport

I am only here to be used

That bitch is through toss her out like dried out salad

Male fungus

Bring you into existence

A woman is to be cherished

Stretch out your hands and grab hold of today

Tomorrow is not reachable

The future can be dreamed

It's Time To Cultivate

Emasculate

Do you hear what I hear?

A gun shot

Do you see what I see?

A whore standing on the bus stop

Do you hear what I hear?

A hungry baby crying

Do you see what I see? *I see... I see*

The stars up high, burning still in the sky

That is a sign that everything is fine

Make a wish

Make a wish make a wish

Make a wish

Make a wish make a wish

He sold dreams

Stole hopes

Just a little dope to smoke

A little ecstasy to slur your speech

You are on cloud nine

Scream, because you have redeemed your vitality

If even for a short reality

On the street corners, ducking in the backseats of cars

J.L.Davenport

Shaking hands with the dope head to deliver
To receive change, in his life
He saw some clothes he wanted when he was 16
He saw some shoes he had to sport when he was 17
He saw a car he had to ride when he was 18
Had to have the jewels and support his girl give his new baby the world when he was 19
22, he got robbed, retaliated, and bobbed a sawed off shotgun in the face of the perpetrating thief who tried to grab hold of his future and run
He sold dreams, stole hopes
He wished he had
Now he is age 23 and 23 hours in a cage
Make a wish
Make a wish make a wish
Make a wish
Make a wish make a wish

She struts her stuff
Hips, butt, and a lot of make up
She don't care about her hair because the men don't care
It is about her derriere and the way she shares her tongue

It's Time To Cultivate

Rubs her gums up and down
Swallows it when they cum

She is in hell, like the burning on her skin from her cheap under wire bra
The small warts that burst, they hurt and itch in a once precious place that is more like a ditch
Been hitched, stitched, stabbed, whipped, and now diseased
She is in hell here
Once a bright kid jumping rope and singing songs
Went from playing doll, tea time and house
To wearing thongs
Got pregnant and life faded away
No more play it is all real and she is alone to deal with the agony
So she denies herself and thinks of the kid
She gambles the highest bid on the streets for the kid
Make a wish make a wish
All about the kid, it is all about the kid
I promise tomorrow that it will be different
That it will get easier, mom says
Tomorrow comes and the baby is not a baby anymore

J.L.Davenport

The baby has answered more doors and gave as much head as its prostituting mother
The baby is now five but has never really been a baby
She now carries a fee that is how she eats
She knows she makes her mommy happy
When her mommy is sleeping, she cries for a toy not a boy
Make a wish make a wish
Do you hear what I hear?
Unnatural cries and screams
Do you see what I see?

It's Time To Cultivate

No One Helped

A night of harmless karaoke gone bad
I sang some beautiful music, some happy, some sad
Did a Tina Turner and Chaka Kahn 'cause I felt like being bad
Hopped off the stage doing a shake your booty dance
A man says, "Why you always come here alone, you know how many men want to take you home?"
I just smiled and said, "I didn't have a date because a lot of men out here don't match my taste."
Then he responds, "That's too bad." and turns to his right looks at another girl and asked her to be his wife.
He buys the pretty girl a free drink
The not so handsome old man says, "The drink is on me."
Her man sits across the room batting his eyes. He cannot even believe the old man really tried.
Instead of determining the truth, he is quick to imply
Looks at his girl questioning, infers that she will

J.L.Davenport

lie about the conversation with the old man, and how she got that drink?
He screams at his girl!
"It's time to go!" the bouncer says, "You won't be doing this mess up in here."
He did not take the embarrassment lightly but he went on his way without any problems, because the only problems were his girl and he would definitely solve them
No one helped her, not even me
He hit her like a man multiple times right over there in the street
People laughed and said oh damn like she was nothing
I ran to my vehicle, locked the doors, and tried to do something
Calling the cops wasn't easy let them come beat a brother down
I did not want to stick around
I was feeling queasy
I came home where I am safe, my desolate place of solitude
Cried in my car two hours or so listening to
love tunes and I think the early Sunday blues
I wonder if that girl was safe or if the cops were to

slow

I doubt I will ever know

No one helped her, not even me

Deprive me of love if I had to deal with that

I would be a dead woman 'cause I would fight back

If I broke every finger, just to break his nose

I would embrace being a tyrant because everything goes

She came to look good, dance, sing and drink with her man

Her man swings her little ass against the car as if it is her last chance for love

I wish I could trade places with her

No I don't...yes I do...hell no

Oh, what is the use?

I still do not feel any better

I am so ashamed

She was so small

Oh the pain

I heard some of those punches and slaps when I ran to my car

I saw him kicking her

I saw men standing around with their mouths wide open

J.L.Davenport

Some smoking cigars full of weed and some were choking
Some were laughing and inciting
(Lord, I am not handling this well, please intervene)
I wished I had a gun or even a bat
I should have used my SUV attempted to scare him and let him chase after me
I am thinking criminal but it don't matter I am home
That girl is alone with that man, her man
I am so hurt I could have done stomach crunches for a week straight and I still would not feel this way
What is wrong with these men?
Same thing that was always wrong
I am guessing
I will be alone forever because I am not feeling them today
Maybe I will cry some more
Maybe I will sit and think
Maybe I will get me some hot tea
Maybe I will cry, think and get me some hot tea
Cause
No one helped her, not even me

NIGGA

Nigga

Nigga

Nigga

Nigga, huh?

I'm a real *Nigga*

That's what you say...

(Silence)

Here is what I say...

Damn straight you's a *Nigga*

Representing inferiority

Continuing the plague of inferiority

Promoting inferiority

Prospering off of demoting your fellow man

Hey *Nigga*, whatchu got in those pants.

A whole lot of shit?

Your ass is rubbing up against your ankles,

dragging your feet *Nigga*

Humph, papa didn't fertilize any *Nigga*

Humph, mama didn't born no *Nigga*

Humph, families didn't raise any *Nigga*

Humph, communities didn't look out for any

Nigga

Where is your culture brother? Do you know from whence you came?

J.L.Davenport

Na you don't know, which is a whole other problem of its own
Just dragging your feet
Living your life uncivilized
Trying to dodge the streets
Dodging the streets don't make you a *Nigga*...*Nigga*
(Silence)
We did not march to have no *Nigga*...brother
We did not die to have no free *Nigga*...brother
We did not slave in the fields to have no *Nigga*...son
We weren't chained on dark, molded, sickness, infested ships to have no *Nigga*...son
Beat...*Nigga*
Hanged...*Nigga*
Cut off that *nigga's* big black balls and stuff them in his monkey lips...*Nigga*
Rape that little nappy-headed wench ruin her insides...*Nigga*
Beat that old coon like a man...*Nigga*
Burn that (*Nigga*)...listen to him scream like a bitch...*Nigga*
(Silence)
They were no *nigga's*

They were strong and brilliant people whose lives were not so simple

Oh wait...but you is a *Nigga*

Ignorance

Shaming yourself

Shaming your lineage, your generation, your brothers and sisters around you...who share your color, your race, past, present and future

Shaming us all with no sense...*Nigga*

Tell me this, what makes *Nigga* ok?

Do not say it is spelled a different way

Do not say, "Damn!" It doesn't even sound the same."

Do not say, "But, I am a *Nigga*."

That one slanged up pain of a word claimed the dignity of a people once and it is a horrid misinterpretation of a people now

Oh wait, but you is a *Nigga*

Humph,

The first *Nigga*, the last *Nigga*, the best *Nigga*, the worse *Nigga*, the realest *Nigga*, the dopest *Nigga*

Nigga with no figure

Humph,

Yes you's a *Nigga*, You's also the betrayed *Nigga*,

J.L.Davenport

the lost *Nigga*, the robbed *Nigga* and I ain't talking about no dope
You's also the shamed *Nigga*, then blamed *Nigga*, hated *Nigga*, incarcerated *Nigga*, mocked *Nigga*, illiterate *Nigga*, rags to riches and back to rags *Nigga*
You's also the laughed at *Nigga* by all them copycat wanting to be *nigga's* and can be *nigga's* if they want to....*Nigga*
So if you like to be all those things *Nigga*... then be a *Nigga*....*Nigga*
Be a *NIGGA* alone

BLACK

BLACK cometh from the dirt

Molded and breathed in

It gave birth to the jewels of this Earth

Once upon a time BLACK was undiscovered, unexplored, unaltered, unabashed and unafraid

Once upon a time BLACK was unharmed, undisturbed, unbroken and unbound

Once upon a time BLACK was unbiased, unblemished, unchanged, and unashamed

Once upon a time BLACK was unmarked, unnamed, unpunished, unrefined, untainted

And unrelated

Wake up child wake up

It is time to cultivate

Yesterday BLACK turned brown

Unaccented, uncultured and lost

Yesterday brown turned yellow

Unconnected, unreadable, unaffiliated and burdened

Yesterday yellow turned beige

Beige turned gray

Today gray turned pale and it is unbelievable

J.L.Davenport

Celebrity

I am a celebrity

How wonderful it is to be a celebrity

Living such prestige, that I have no peace

No moment alone

No moment of rest

No moment not shown

No moment, not heard

Even within the walls of my home

I am a celebrity

No one sees me for who I am or what I use to be

I am forever this celebrity or I am nobody

Drunk

Drunk do you think you are hiding?

You see yourself clearly with every taste and so do we see you

Drunk do you hear the wail?

It is the grief coming to slap you double

The taste has dissolved into bitter your breath as harsh as manures pile

Your tears are not of salt but of bodily fluids

In your eyes are challenge and pain

Your body pleasure

God will grace your tongue one hundred times and ain't nobody listening

J.L.Davenport

Recreate This Image

Get rid of that wet pillowcase and dry your tears
Find a refrigerator and make your thighs big
Recreate this image in your mind
An unfortunate problem of these times
Do not let the breeze brush you with clean fresh air
Have a menthol cigarette long and lasting
Recreate this image in your mind
An unfortunate problem of these times
An erection pinpoints its pleasures
Walking smiling lips foaming never close
Recreate this image in your mind
An unfortunate problem of these times
Whip you; choke you, grope and scream
Sometimes she sees demons
Can we blame her?
The father again is missing
Recreate this image in your mind
An unfortunate problem of these times
Lose the adrenaline rush from pure exertion
You can get an X-pill for twenty dollars but it is illegal
However, if you go to your health shop you can buy for thirty dollars equals ninety days of all the ephedrine you need and not only will you be high

and moving fast but also the weight will drop quickly

Recreate this image in your mind

An unfortunate problem of these times

Mona Lisa the purest beauty

The average woman is ugly

Recreate this image

J.L.Davenport

Mask of Beauty

Concealed deep within

Between the layers of skin, fat, and veins is a mask of beauty so deprived of life

Dehydrated of love

Overflowing with life's stresses and pains

The trickery of thy mirror

Thy only comfort, thy truest torturer

Who is the most beautiful of them all?

Who is the fairest and who shall fall?

Am I fat or surely thin?

Another wrinkle, blemishing, once young, smooth, skin

Give me back my shine and zest!

Is thy plumpness drooping in my chest?

Nothing is viler than a beauty that stirs the sight

Though inside lingers disorder.

Give up self

Wake up every morning to give up self to the world for a whole day

Everyday

Cry out in me

I allow your stresses, your pains, your agitations, depressions, humiliations, and strains

Cry out in me for release, a meditative seclusion is sometimes the solution

I the lifting shoulders and warm arms

I the soft voice

I the musical heart

I the thick pockets to be emptied

The heavy eyes with no sleep

The dizzy head

The swollen feet

I who give up self, which is everything

To allow others peace

J.L.Davenport

Suffer Blessed One

Just waking up is a blessing
Your life is no doubt the very essence of blessed art
thou the chemistry of Gods making
I too shall suffer

Reflection

The seas of the Heavens have opened.
With it comes the anguish and ridicule.
Gaze; my reflection is faltering through the
aftermath, of a hard pouring rain.
As sober as it is, its slippery stain does not show
the intensity or the humility dripping off my nose.
My serene reflection wrinkles away to another's
puddle. My puddle has darkened now. My
reflection is now belligerent. My reflection is lost
and in despair, my reflection is where?
I am still gazing though my reflection has
diminished and is not clear
I am still gazing
my eyes have left the puddle
they look to the Heavens, the Heavens that opened
so briefly to be so destructing.
Then there is ease for something whispered," I am

tired and this world is unclean..."

Then there is ease possibly the reflection of old testaments? Possibly

One extra sprinkle from the Heavens to fertilize my weakened stance can hold me back. However, in the sprinkle will be a mirror and in that mirror, unblemished and clear, shows a blossoming spring forthcoming, with me in it.

My reflection will return.

Smiling and at ease.

Unique

I have many unique gifts

Unique gifts that I cannot share because in this world my unique gifts are a monstrosity

I have many unique gifts, unique gifts that I cannot give because there is no one as multi unique as me to receive the blessing

Somehow, the pleasures of this world have taken shape

Seducing out morality

Virtue is weak

One must demoralize their body

(Let my body sing for me)

Voice has no voice

Lyrics have no meaning

If they did, they are not heard anyway

Lost in the bass, the repetition, the screams

No perfect lines if you are blind

Just time, touch and Braille

Even through sight you do not see

Spirit lost inside a shell, even with a story to tell

Bring me down to my knees

My written words are not read

My written words are not fantasized

Ok I just lied

Nevertheless, today people still cannot read and if they could, they do not comprehend

I have many unique gifts that I cannot share nor give

I am just a dreamer in a hustler's world

Unique don't cut it

To be or not to be is the mentality

To lie and cheat is the reality

Did my father molest me, my brother rape me? Hell no!

However, if they did I would probably be closer to being a headline and closer to a dream in this hustler's world

Maybe my mother should have been a crack head

It's Time To Cultivate

on the hoe stroll with next lifetime on her mind
I could have used her as an excuse to be lose and fuck my way to a dream
A hustler would agree there is no other use for me
Maybe I should get my breast over inflated with sacs of man-blessed juices
How will I look to you then?
Some liposuction to my knees, then I could bend low, all the way to the floor and leave my knee prints behind
Half size my genetically big butt
Remove one or two ribs
Get my nose trimmed to a nostril
Reduce my pigmentation
Get lip inflation until they are an ass on my face
How will I sound to you then?
A hustler would agree there is no other use for me
Better to be a freak than be unique
I stand-alone artistically blessed while others prosper off stupidity
I am unique
This world is not ready for me

J.L.Davenport

Happiness Won't Come To You

You have nothing

The price you will have to pay

For the good ones in your life you treat the worse way

All the pity you endow upon yourself

Is the time consume of someone else

The using, cheating, mistreatments, selfish and greedy

You have learned no lesson

Another will take you for the same ride

Pity you, hustler to another

Happiness will not come to you

He Made Me Feel

Is it a crime to have such beauty, smile, style and intelligence?

Is it a crime to allow a man to want, to need, to dream, to fantasize?

Is it a crime to be able, even with child or children to overt a man and drive him wild?

Some will say yes and man won't understand why he feels, why he lust, why he needs

Why he made you feel like you were nothing

Why he made us feel like we were nothing

Why he made me feel like I was nothing

With child? He asked.

Then he replied.

With the look in his eyes

Desperate to hide

That he was surprised

From a wonderful day went the moment

As tears swelled up in my eyes

This man came to me and I was genuinely friendly

and because he assumed quite the contrary

He made me feel like nothing

I wish...I wish... it was I before him

The man would say

We could have been the perfect couple

J.L.Davenport

I wish...I wish... I had met you back when
Nevertheless, he meets me now and then puts me down
You are so beautiful, you are intelligent and your approach is so sweet and innocent
But you have kids
He made you feel like you were nothing
He made us feel like we were nothing
He made me feel like I was nothing

Kids Sing

Listening to the kids sing, "when I die I'm going to heaven and I'll still be alive," la la La la... they do not know what they sing
I was a child once
Someone stole that from me
If I could clock my heels
1
2
3
And have it all again
That would be peace

It's Time To Cultivate

Last Cry

The violins are playing
I never thought I would know when it was time to go
Whoever has the chance to say they'd really know?
I think I have had all the say that I am going to say
I am broke anyways so any good it has done
The phone does not ring anymore
No knuckles collapse against my door
It is just me alone
Been alone for a long time
Even through pain
Rape
Child
Rape
Childbirth
Abuse
Misuse
Disease
Childbirth
Starvation
Manipulation
Childbirth
Beatings
Isolation

J.L. Davenport

Corrections
Self-buildup
Who says a man cannot keep you down?
Well they can and they will
Build you up and then knock you the other way
until there is no direction to turn but disperse
Even in search for good do they hurt you
Today I step down
Too hard to wear the crown and wear it
It hurts
Serenity is in the plastic
Even the commercial says so nature's gift
Goodbye
The quiet will be good for me
It is all I have ever known
The violins are playing

CHAPTER 3
Sight, Sound, and Music

J.L.Davenport

True Art

Beauty is in the eye of the one who sees it

It is an expression of art

God created many beauties

The female being most prized

The male he gave the eyes

To admire his jewels

To honor and cherish

To protect and serve

As in God, we owe them the world

And the universe and the stars if only to reach them

For they are the lock which was opened to release the fruit of our being

Our being is to fertilize the many gifts they have to offer

Music

Inward music

Outward music

We're all dancing and singing

Rapping or rocking

Never less, it is the luminous of who we are

By far, it is the aura of our spirits, which keeps us

going

Music soothes the mind, brings comfort to thy soul and warmth to thy heart

Harmony, groove, roll, and soul

Good Morning

Good morning sunrise

Hello to the sunlight, the blue horizon is my pillow

There is nothing more precious to me than a new day on my waking

It is all that I am happy to see...so breathtaking

The music transcends from you

My morning yawn into a shower song

Even the birds are singing your tune

The natural aromas

The foggy air

Crowding the sleepy moon

"Wake up Moon and go to bed."

Its morning

Its morning

Its morning

Good morning, blue sky

Goodbye to the stars that hide and the slobber in the craters Moon

Its morning

Thunderous Music

So beautiful this music

Strong and passionate

The smoothness

So sensuous the chorus

The horn swings

Moans

Rapture

The trombone blows

Strong

The drums strength

Beats

Pouncing over and over

Delicately yet strongly

Vibrating against the walls

Gradually becoming sweet

Echoing its bass

So emotional the violins come into play

Gently light bodied

Soft

Hollow inside

Angelic strings penetrated

Massaged and elevated

Strenuous

It's Time To Cultivate

Shaking light vibes

The piano alone

Thick boned

High

Low

Watcher

Listener

One with the fingers

Hitting the "g" awaiting full attention punching it gently

Lengthening the arrival of a loud thunderous recital

Swaying

Swelling

Soprano

Tenor

Alto

Unison

Orgasmic

Sounds of music

J.L.Davenport

Dance

Ecstasy loomed off the dancers

The heat and steam gloomed on their foreheads

Budded and clasped in their armpits

Squeaked between their buttocks

Leaked and lingered on their genitals

Pheromones of passion

The motion

The charisma

The enticing imagination from their teasing bodies

The flaming dance

Compilation

Feel the Pain

Do da da de da da de do
I want you to feel the pain
Hear it see it
I am tired of other people's pain
I am tired of carrying people's troubles and feeling all their pain
I am frustrated, saturated, suffocating in other peoples fucking pain
Do you hear what I hear? A gun shot
Do you see what I see? A young whore standing on the bus stop
Do you hear what I hear? A hungry baby crying
Do you see what I see, I see, I see
The stars up high burning in the still dark sky, is a sign that everything is fine
Make a wish
He sold dreams and stole hopes, just a little dope to smoke
Some ecstasy, some weed, and acid… whatever you need
Scream cause you're on cloud number
Muthafuckin nine, you've redeemed your vitality for a short reality

J.L.Davenport

On the street corners, ducking into cars
Whatchu need? What's cracking?
To receive change in his life
He saw some clothes he wanted when he was 16
(*y'all like that!*)
He saw some shoes he had to sport when he was
17 (*because I got it like that!*)
He saw a truck he had to ride when he was 18
Had to have the jewels and the girls
Then give his baby the world when he was 19
Twenty-two he was robbed
Retaliated and fired a sawed off shotgun into the
face of the thief leaving the gun at his feet
The fingerprints remain along with his name hmm
DNA is the same, only one to blame
Just a little dope to smoke, some ecstasy, some
weed… whatever you need
Need a new identity cause now 23 and 23 hours in
a cell definitely aware he'll be old as hell before he
will leave there and that is if he can survive the
prison butchers stolen kitchen knives
The prison guards crooked insight
The sexually depressed, mind regressed prisoners
fondling their loins in his ass
He is sitting in his jail cell living day after day

It's Time To Cultivate

creating wigs from his own pubic hair
Miniskirts from soiled pillowcases
Have to be somebody's bitch to escape a deadly fate
Trying to distant himself from realization of damnation and find Jesus
It is heaven that he thinks of… but he's going to hell
He was born free *(free like… free like)*
Yet he is not free
However, until he is free he will not rest
Although rest will come only in death for he, and still he will not be free
It is heaven that he thinks of… but he's going to hell
Thomas A. Dorsey wrote, *Take my hand precious Lord…* yet as this prisoner sings this song of faith and will his fingertips are stale
The moisture against his palms aren't from the mist of perspirations but from the leaking girth of his cellmates yearning
Nothing like being a man in a man's world
He yearns for freedom
With a strain and a sigh he falls to sleep, wondering is this the night he will die

J.L.Davenport

With a strain and a sigh he awakens in the morning, wondering is this the day he will die
To be buried in the freedom for sale plot on the government lot
Make a wish
She struts her stuff
Hips, butt and a lot of makeup
She don't care about her hair because the men don't care
Just switch and pop that derriere let that negligee swing
Share those lips and that tongue
As long as she rubs, those gums up and down no teeth but a smile
Swallows it when they cum
The last drip from that mushroomed tip sliding through her lips
She is in hell here, like the burning on her skin from her cheap, dirty under wire
Bra
The small warts that burst, they hurt and itch in a once precious place that is more like a ditch
Been hitched, stabbed, stitched, raped, and now diseased
Maybe she should just give her life to Jesus

because *God uses ordinary people*
Once a bright kid jumping rope with so much hope
Singing songs, playing doll, tea time and house
Directing invisible choirs and mimicking the adult choir songs, *Use me O Lord*
Now she wears thongs, what a wonderful thing
Goes to house parties, takes drugs and gets gang banged… do your thing sweet thing
Got pregnant and life faded away
No more play it is all real and she is alone to deal with the agony of the corner
So she denies herself and thinks of the kid
She gambles her life on the streets for the kid
Make a wish
All about the kid it is all about the kid
I promise tomorrow that it will be different
That it will get easier
Tomorrow comes and the baby is not a baby anymore just a sad case of pain and broken promises, a little girl lost to the world, five years old and lost to the world
She has opened more doors and gave as much head as her prostituting mother
She now carries a fee that is how she eats

J.L.Davenport

Every night she cries herself to sleep dreaming of toys not boys
Listening to the melody of her mother's bed squeak
Make a wish make a fucking wish
Do you hear what I hear? Do you see what I see?
Do you hear the pain I see? Do you see that pain I hear? A lot of pain

It's Time To Cultivate

! Get To Know!
J.L.Davenport

https://www.facebook.com/author.jldavenport

J.L. Davenport is a spoken word artist, author and songwriter.

It's Time To Cultivate

www.ingramcontent.com/pod-product-compliance
Lightning Source LLC
Chambersburg PA
CBHW031420040426
42444CB00005B/657